Copyrighted Mater

IBIZA
TRAVEL GUIDE

The Most Recent Pocket Guide to the Island of Bliss | Explore the Hidden Charms, Vibrant Nightlife, and Idyllic Escapes of Ibiza

FLORENCE THOMAS

Copyrighted Material

Copyright© 2023 Florence Thomas

All rights reserved. No part of this publication may be reproduced, distributed, or transmitted in any form or by any means, including photocopying, recording, or other electronic or mechanical methods, without the prior written permission of the publisher, except in the case of brief quotations embodied in critical reviews and certain other noncommercial uses permitted

Copyrighted Material

Table Of Content

INTRODUCTION   5
  Map Of Ibiza   8
  Ibiza City Image   9
CHAPTER 1 : INTRODUCTION   10
  My Personal Experience   10
  The Allure Of Ibiza   18
  The Guide's Objectives   23
CHAPTER 2 : Historical and Cultural Insights   28
  Historical Background Of Ibiza   28
  Cultural Highlights and Traditions   34
  The Geography Of Ibiza   40
  Essential Travel Phrases   43
CHAPTER 3 : PREPARING FOR YOUR TRIP   47
  Planning Your Journey   47
  What you need to Know About Ibiza   53
  Essential Information for Visitors   59
  Budgeting For Your Ibiza Adventure   65
  How to get to Ibiza   69
  Best Time to Visit Ibiza   73
  Local Customs and Etiquette   78
CHAPTER 4 : LODGING AND ACCOMMODATIONS 83
  Welcome to Ibiza   83
  Arriving In Ibiza   88

Copyrighted Material

Language and Communication Tips	91
Best Places to Stay In Ibiza	96
1. Town of Ibiza (Eivissa):	96
2. The beach of the Bossa:	97
3. San Antoni de Portmany (San Antonio):	100
4. Saint Eulalia des Riu:	100
5. Ibiza's interior	101
An Overview of Accommodation Options	102
CHAPTER 5 : NAVIGATING IBIZA	108
Getting Around the Island	108
The Top Places to Visit in Ibiza	115
1. Ibiza Town's Dalt Vila	115
2. The Es Vedrà	117
6. Nevada City:	118
7. Saint Eulalia des Riu:	119
CALLA COMETE	119
Formentera:	120
Bay of San Antonio:	120
Hippy Market and Es Canar:	121
Exploring the Beautiful Beaches	122
1. The beach of the Bossa:	123
2. Cala Comte (Cala Conta)	123
4. Jondal, Cala:	123
5. Cala Salada as well as Cala Saladeta:	124
6. Playa de Ses Salines, Ses Salines:	125

Copyrighted Material

7. Cala Vadella	125
8. Xarraca, Cala:	125
Exciting Tours And Activities: Boat Trips	127
Rural Hotels and Rustic Retreats	133
Sampling the Local Culinary Delights	138

CHAPTER 6 : EXPERIENCING IBIZA'S NIGHTLIFE AND ENTERTAINMENT — 144

Dinning and Gastronomic Experiences	144
The Best Clubs for Nightlife Enthusiasm	148
Enjoying The Quaint Bars	155
Ibiza for Families: Enjoyable for Everyone	159
Embracing Sustainable Tourism Practices	162

CHAPTER 7 : OUTDOOR ADVENTURES IN IBIZA — 166

Engaging In Outdoor Activities	167
Discovering Hidden Gems and Secret Spots	171

CHAPTER 8 : EXPLORING IBIZA'S NATURAL BEAUTY — 175

Chasing Stunning Sunsets	176
Visiting Picturesque Villages	180
Unveiling The Regions Of Ibiza	184

CHAPTER 9 : WORTH A SPECIAL TRIP — 192

Hidden Treasures Of Ibiza	192
Special Qualities and Attractions	196

CONCLUSION : EMBRACING THE IBIZA EXPERIENCE — 202

Final Thoughts on the Allure of Ibiza	202

Copyrighted Material

Sustainable and Responsible tourism in Ibiza 203

Advice for a Memorable Journey   204

INTRODUCTION

Welcome to the enchanting shores of Ibiza, a paradise that beckons all wanderers seeking an unforgettable adventure! Dive into the latest edition of the "Ibiza Travel Guide 2023 2024," meticulously curated to unleash the magic and splendor of this sun-kissed Mediterranean gem. Discover pristine beaches adorned with turquoise waters, explore the vibrant nightlife that pulsates through the island, and immerse yourself in the rich cultural tapestry woven through its ancient towns.

Get ready to embrace the essence of Ibiza – an experience like no other awaits!

Copyrighted Material

Map Of Ibiza

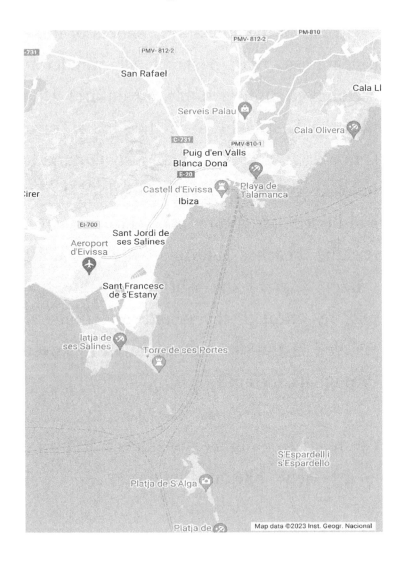

Ibiza City Image

Copyrighted Material

CHAPTER 1 : **INTRODUCTION**

My Personal Experience

Welcome to the Ibiza Travel Guide, where I chronicle my travels and adventures on the beautiful island of Ibiza. I had the honor of visiting Ibiza for four unforgettable days, which forever changed the way my heart and soul felt about travel. This part will give you a peek at the beauty that awaits you on this exquisite island by walking you through the nicest locations I saw, including the gorgeous beaches, elegant hotels, delicious restaurants, and more.

When I first arrived in Ibiza, I was enthralled by the island's alluring vibe.

The island's distinctive fusion of history, culture, and breathtaking natural beauty produces a mood that is both energizing and peaceful.

I found myself immersed in a world of varied experiences that suited every aspect of my wanderlust as I toured the island.

Beaches:

Ibiza is well known for the immaculate beaches that adorn its coastline. I had the opportunity to see some of the most stunning beaches when I was there. Each beach provided something different, whether it was relaxing on the fine beaches, swimming in the beautiful seas, or engaging in thrilling water sports.

The lively Playa d'en Bossa, the serene Cala Conta with its breathtaking sunset views, and the isolated Cala Salada, where nature's splendor seemed unspoiled and otherworldly, were some of my favorites.I deliberately chose lodgings that exactly fit the appeal of Ibiza so that I could genuinely engage in the spirit of the island. Every hotel, from opulent coastal resorts to basic lodges in the countryside, provided a distinctive experience.

I found myself savoring the first-rate facilities, first-rate service, and breathtaking balcony views. A more personal and genuine relationship with the island's culture was also made possible by the wonderful atmosphere of the boutique hotels located in Ibiza's tiny towns.

Gastronomy and restaurants

The gastronomic scene in Ibiza is a foodie's heaven. I had delicious dinners made using fresh, regional products during my whole stay. Each restaurant offered an international flavor experience, as well as typical Spanish fare, that thrilled my taste buds. The lively ambiance of coastal chiringuitos (beach bars) and the elegant flair of fine dining establishments enhanced the magical eating experiences.

Memorable Moments:

One special memory from my stay in Ibiza sticks out above all the others: the spellbinding sunset at Es Vedrà. Off the southwest coast of Ibiza, there is an uninhabited rock island that is well-known for its magical aura and attraction.

I was overcome with a feeling of tranquility and amazement as the sun started to set, painting the sky with vivid orange and pink colors.

I will always remember it as a perfect blissful moment.

Living the Ibiza's Life :

I was able to sense the beat of the island and engage with its colorful culture throughout my four days in Ibiza. Every moment was equally exciting and peaceful, whether it was dancing to the pounding rhythms of renowned clubs or exploring the beautiful countryside.

The island's charm was further enhanced by the warmth and friendliness of the islanders, who made me feel at home and ease.

In this travel guide, I try to capture the spirit of my own Ibiza experience by sharing tips on where to go, what to look for while traveling, and other aspects of the island's allure.

Ibiza offers something special to offer every tourist, whether they are an adventurer looking for outdoor thrills, a history buff wanting to discover old ruins, a foodie wanting to indulge in gourmet pleasures, or a soul looking for peace amid nature's beauty.

So join me as we explore Ibiza's attractions, a place where dreams are realized and amazing memories are created.

The Allure Of Ibiza

Ibiza, the captivating pearl of the Mediterranean, lures visitors from all over the world with its alluring charm. This little Balearic island, often known as the White Isle, is renowned for its exciting nightlife, gorgeous beaches, fascinating cultural heritage, and rich history.

Beyond being known as a party island, Ibiza has a variety of charms that draw visitors from all walks of life looking for an experience they won't soon forget.

Natural Beauty

Ibiza's stunning natural beauty is one of its main attractions. The island is a haven for environment lovers, from its beautiful beaches with fine sand and clear seas to its craggy cliffs and dense pine woods.

There are many chances for exploration and outdoor activities due to the variety of sceneries, which range from tranquil rural settings to stunning coastline panoramas.

Nightlife Entertainment

Ibiza has established a reputation as the world's party capital by drawing renowned DJs and revelers to its beachside clubs.

There is no other nightlife like it, with thrilling parties that last into the wee hours of the morning and world-class music events.

The island also has stylish sunset bars, live music venues, and cultural events that highlight its thriving arts scene for visitors looking for a more relaxed experience.

Culture and History

Ibiza has a rich historical legacy that dates back thousands of years in addition to its hedonistic appeal. The Phoenicians, Romans, Moors, and Catalans were just a few of the civilizations that formed the island and left behind an amazing tapestry of cultural influences. Ibiza's historic landmarks—ancient ruins, old churches, and walled citadels—invite tourists to learn more about the island's interesting past.

Gastronomy

Fresh fish, regional vegetables, and traditional Spanish cuisine make up Ibiza's culinary scene, which is a celebration of Mediterranean tastes. The island's cuisine mixes the bounty of the land and the sea, and it provides a fantastic selection of eateries, seaside chiringuitos, and farm-to-table experiences. The wide variety of delicious options will excite the taste buds of food lovers.

Sustainable travel and ethical tourism

Ibiza has made great progress in the last several years toward eco-friendly tourist methods to protect its natural beauty and rich cultural history for future generations. The island's concept has included eco-friendly programs, sustainable lodgings, and environmental protection activities. Travelers may actively participate in sustainable tourism, helping to protect Ibiza's priceless treasures.

The Guide's Objectives

The Ibiza Travel Guide's main goals are to improve visitors' experiences on the island by giving them thorough and reliable information. These are the goals of this manual:

Copyrighted Material

1. _Comprehensive Information_: The book aims to cover a broad variety of themes, from historical and cultural background to useful travel advice. It aims to be a one-stop shop for comprehensive information on the island, accommodating a range of interests and travel inclinations.

2. _Unique Insights and Personal Experiences:_ The guide strives to give unique insights and personal experiences in addition to factual information, enabling readers to relate to the author's journey and enthusiasm for Ibiza. These tales will provide a more vivid and captivating view of the island's appeal.

3. *Integration of Sustainable and Responsible Tourism:* The guide will emphasize eco-friendly practices, responsible travel alternatives, and efforts that promote environmental preservation and cultural appreciation in recognition of the significance of sustainable tourism.

4. *Engaging Writing:* By avoiding too technical terminology or jargon, the book aims to be user-friendly and accessible. Readers of diverse backgrounds will find this book to be pleasant due to its engaging style and complex terminology.

5. *User-Friendly Format:* The guide will be set up in a user-friendly format with clear headings, subheadings, and an extensive

index for rapid reference. This will facilitate navigation.

By achieving these goals, the Ibiza Travel Guide hopes to become a reliable resource for tourists, enabling them to make choices, find hidden treasures, and construct lifelong memories on the alluring island of Ibiza.

CHAPTER 2 : Historical and Cultural Insights

Historical Background Of Ibiza

Ibiza is one of the oldest communities in the western Mediterranean, nestled in the blue waters of the Mediterranean Sea and with a history that stretches back thousands of years. A complex tapestry of cultural influences that have shaped Ibiza's character today has been left behind by many civilizations throughout the millennia due to the island's strategic position, fertile soil, and natural ports.

Pre Historic Settlement

Ibiza may have been inhabited as early as 3000 BCE during the Bronze Age, according to archaeological findings.

The Talaiotic people, an old prehistoric civilization that left behind remarkable megalithic structures including talaiots (watchtowers), navetas (burial chambers), and hypogeums (subterranean graves), were probably the island's initial residents. There are still several archaeological sites where you may study these relics of the island's ancient history.

Carthaginian and Phoenician Influence:

The Phoenicians, an early maritime culture from the eastern Mediterranean, established trade ports on Ibiza about the 7th century BCE. The island's natural riches, particularly its salt, a prized commodity, drew them in.

The Phoenicians contributed their language and habits, adding to the island's cultural fusion.

Ibiza's Greek name, "Ibossim," is derived from the Phoenician phrase "Ibossim" or "Yboshim," which means "island of the god Bes."

Ibiza was subjugated by the Carthaginians, a former maritime force with a base in modern-day Tunisia, in the fifth century BCE. Ibiza prospered as a hub of trade and commerce in the western Mediterranean throughout the Carthaginian era. Ibosim, also known as Ebusus in Latin, was founded by the Carthaginians and subsequently served as the Roman province of Hispania's capital.

Roman Domination:

Ibiza came under Roman control in 123 BCE during the Second Punic War.

The Romans understood the strategic value of the ports on the island and its potential as a significant commercial center. As it developed into a crucial stop on the maritime trade routes connecting Rome to other Mediterranean locations, Ibiza's economic prosperity expanded. The ruins of palaces, baths, and roadways that may still be discovered on the island are clear indications of Roman influence.

The Byzantine era and the conquest of the Muslims

In the sixth century CE, Ibiza was ruled by the Byzantines after the collapse of the Western Roman Empire.

But many Germanic tribes often invaded and raided the island.

Finally, in the eighth century, the North African Moors took control of Ibiza, ushering in the era of the Muslims.

Ibiza had a strong and long-lasting Islamic impact. The Moors left a lasting impression on the island's architectural and cultural customs in addition to bringing new agricultural methods and better irrigation systems. In Ibiza's architectural and cultural legacy, one can still see the distinct blending of Moorish and Spanish traditions.

Cristian Reconquest and Later Years:

Ibiza was successfully taken by Christian soldiers led by King James I of Aragon and

Catalonia in 1235, putting the island under Christian dominion.

The island joined the Kingdom of Aragon when the Christian invaders gradually integrated the native populace.

Due to economic hardships and pirate invasions, Ibiza went through phases of prosperity and downfall throughout the next decades. The island saw some relative stability throughout the 18th century, and agriculture, fishing, and marine commerce helped to revive its economy.

With its ancient ruins, historic cathedrals, and customary festivals preserving the heritage of the many civilizations that formerly called the island home, Ibiza serves as a living witness to its rich past today.

In addition to taking in the island's contemporary attractions and lively culture, visitors to Ibiza have the rare chance to learn more about this intriguing historical backdrop.

Cultural Highlights and Traditions

Ancient customs, contemporary influences, and a thriving arts scene are all woven together in a mesmerizing way in Ibiza's cultural tapestry. The island's distinctive cultural landmarks and customs add to its attractiveness by giving tourists a rich experience that goes beyond its image as a party island.

Here are a few of the major customs and cultural landmarks that make Ibiza unique:

1. Culture of Ibibio:

The indigenous inhabitants of the island, referred to as "Ibicencos," take great satisfaction in maintaining their traditional way of life, which is firmly based on the island's history and surrounding environment. In Ibicenco culture, the values of family, community, and environmental respect are highly valued.

Visitors will experience the real kindness and warm hospitality of the inhabitants, who will make them feel at home and welcomed by the spirit of the island.

2. Celebrations & Festivals:

Ibiza hosts a variety of exciting festivals and events throughout the year that provide a window into the island's rich cultural legacy. The "Fiesta de la Tierra" (Festival of the Earth), which is celebrated on August 8th and honors the island's customs and rural beginnings, is one of the most important events. During these celebrations, there are vibrant parades, folk dances, and musical performances.

3. Traditional Architecture:

Ibiza's architecture displays the city's history and the different cultures that have influenced it. The island is known for its picturesque whitewashed homes with flat roofs and courtyards in the Moorish style.

The old stone homes with distinctive Sabina wood ceilings may still be seen in certain rural locations. To keep the island's distinctive character, the old architecture must be preserved.

4. Local Craft and Artisans

Ibiza is home to a large population of artists and craftsmen who create handcrafted ceramics, woven baskets, and embroidered fabrics, among other traditional handicrafts. Travelers may see the beauty and craftsmanship that have been handed down through the years by exploring local marketplaces and workshops.

5. Music and Dance:

Ibiza has a rich musical past that includes traditional folk music and dance in addition to its well-known electronic music scene.

Copyrighted Material

A mesmerizing traditional dance known as "ball pagès" is performed at celebratory events and has ornate costumes and rhythmic motions that honor the island's agricultural roots.

6. Culinary Traditions :

Ibiza's cultural heritage has a significant impact on its cuisine. Fresh ingredients from the area are used in traditional meals, along with seafood and Mediterranean-inspired tastes. Tourists may enjoy local specialties like "bullit de peix" (fish stew) and "flaó" (a cheese and mint dessert).

The Geography Of Ibiza

Ibiza, which is located in the western Mediterranean Sea, is one of the Balearic Islands, along with Mallorca, Menorca, and Formentera.

The island, which has a total size of around 572 square kilometers (221 square miles), has a diversified terrain that adds to its allure and natural beauty.

1. Coastal Beauty

The picturesque coastline of Ibiza is well-known for combining cliffs, undiscovered coves, and sandy beaches.

The island's beaches are among the most beautiful in the Mediterranean, drawing both sunbathers and fans of water sports.

Copyrighted Material

Every beach, from the vivacious Playa d'en Bossa to the serene Cala Salada, has its atmosphere.

2. Pre-Forested Hills

Rolling hills covered in dense pine woods characterize Ibiza's interior.

These woods provide countless chances for hiking, mountain biking, and exploring nature paths, and they give a welcome contrast to the coastal vistas. In the center of the island, the aroma of pine and the chattering of cicadas foster a tranquil and calming environment.

3. Agricultural Land

Despite being known as a party island, Ibiza has a large agricultural sector.

Numerous crops, such as olive trees, almond trees, carob trees, and vineyards, may be grown on the rich soil.

Rural areas of the island are filled with old-fashioned farms and lovely landscapes.

6. Natural reserves and Protected Areas :

Ibiza has created several natural reserves and protected areas to preserve its biodiversity and unique ecosystems. The salt flats and birds of the Ses Salines Natural Park, a UNESCO World Heritage site, are well-known.

Because of the island's dedication to conservation, its natural beauty will endure for many more centuries.

Essential Travel Phrases

Learning a few key travel expressions in Spanish before departing for Ibiza will improve your trip and allow you to interact with the locals.

These words and phrases are helpful:

1. Hello: Hola (oh-lah)

2. Good morning: Buenos días (bway-nos dee-ahs)

3. Good afternoon/evening: Buenas tardes (bway-nas tar-days)

4. Goodnight: Buenas noches (bway-nas no-chess)

5. Please: Por favor (por fah-vor)

6. Thank you: Gracias (gra-see-ahs)

7. Yes: Sí (see)

8. No: No (noh)

9. Excuse me/pardon me: Perdón/Disculpe (pair-dohn/dees-kool-peh)

10. I don't understand: No entiendo (noh en-tyen-doh)

11. Do you speak English?: ¿Habla inglés? (ah-blah een-glays)

12. Where is...?: ¿Dónde está...? (don-deh es-tah)

13. How much is this?: ¿Cuánto cuesta esto? (kwahn-toh kways-tah es-toh)

14. I need help: Necesito ayuda (neh-theh-see-toh ah-yoo-dah)

15. Can you recommend a good restaurant?: ¿Puede recomendar un buen restaurante? (pweh-deh reh-koh-men-dar oon bwehn res-tow-rahn-teh)

Understanding and using these fundamental terms can not only improve communication but also show that you appreciate the local way of life. The Ibicencos are kind and value guests who try to adopt their language and traditions.

CHAPTER 3 : PREPARING FOR YOUR TRIP

Planning Your Journey

The right planning is required to ensure a smooth and comfortable visit to Ibiza, the enchanted White Isle. From picking the best time to visit to setting up travel plans, careful preparation lays the groundwork for a fantastic vacation. Here are important steps to remember when you plan your vacation to Ibiza:

1. Choosing the Right Time to Visit:

Ibiza has a Mediterranean climate, which has warm summers and pleasant winters. The peak travel season is from May through September when the weather is lovely and ideal for beach activities and nightlife.

If you're looking for a more leisurely and affordable vacation, think about going in April-May and September-October. The serene wintertime offers a wonderful glimpse into island culture and existence.

2. Obtaining Travel Documents

A minimum of six months should elapse between the expiration of your passport and the period you want to stay in Ibiza. Depending on your nationality, you may additionally need to get a visa to visit Spain. Verify the visa requirements well in advance and apply for any necessary documentation to avoid problems at the last minute.

3. Booking Flights and Accommodations:

After choosing your travel dates, book your flights to Ibiza.

The island's international airport, Ibiza Airport (IBZ), provides frequent flights to significant European cities. To guarantee you have the best accommodation options, consider planning your trip well in advance, especially during the busiest seasons of the year.

Ibiza offers a wide range of accommodation choices, including lavish resorts, charming guesthouses, boutique hotels, and reasonably priced hostels.

4. Looking at the Transportation Option:

Discover the options for traveling on the island. Ibiza has a well-developed public transportation system that comprises buses that connect the island's major towns and popular tourist destinations.

Renting a car or a scooter is another popular option for those who prefer the freedom to explore at their own pace, especially in farther-flung areas.

5. Health and safety Precautions

To prioritize your health and safety, make sure you have complete travel insurance that covers unexpected circumstances and medical emergencies.

It is advisable to discuss any necessary vaccinations or safety precautions with your doctor before traveling.

6. Budgeting and Currency

Create a travel budget that includes spending for housing, transportation, meals, activities, and any other expenses.

The official currency of Spain is the Euro (EUR). Consider carrying both cash and credit cards for convenience, and keep an eye on international exchange rates.

7. Language and cultural awareness

Even though English is often spoken in tourist areas, learning a few basic Spanish phrases may be useful and may enhance your experience. Learn about local customs and etiquette to show respect for Ibiza's cultural heritage.

8. Packing Essentials

Your packing list for the season should include casual clothing, beachwear, and a few dressier options for nightlife and restaurants.

Remember to include a reusable water bottle, sunscreen, a hat, sunglasses, and other essentials.

By carefully planning your vacation, you can make the most of your time in Ibiza and create memorable memories of this enchanting Mediterranean treasure.

What you need to Know About Ibiza

Before immersing yourself in the beautiful island of Ibiza, learn crucial information that might enhance your travel experience. Knowing the nuances of the island, from its various beauty to its cultural norms, will make your trip more pleasurable.

Here's all you need to know about Ibiza:

1. Geography and Regions:

Ibiza is a very small island, with dimensions of around 15 km (9 mi) in breadth and 41 km (25 mi). It is a part of the Balearic archipelago and is located 79 kilometers (49 miles) off the eastern coast of Spain. The five municipalities that make up the island are Ibiza Town (Eivissa), San Antonio (Sant

Antoni de Portmany), Santa Eulària des Riu, San José (Sant Josep de sa Talaia), and San Juan (Sant Joan de Labritja). Every location offers unique activities and attractions.

2. Local Cuisine

Ibiza's cuisine is a lovely fusion of Mediterranean and traditional Spanish dishes. Olive oil, local herbs, fresh fruit, and seafood are major culinary influences on the island.

Ibiza has a vibrant dining scene with a range of cuisines to suit diverse tastes. Don't forget to try regional specialties like "bullit de peix" (fish stew), "sofrit pagès" (beef and vegetable stew), and the well-known dessert "flaó."

3. Nightlife and clubs :

Ibiza is well-known for having incredible nightlife that attracts revelers from all over the globe to its famous clubs and DJs. The island, which hosts some of the priciest parties and concerts, is well known for its electronic dance music (EDM). The two main areas where the nightlife is centered are Ibiza Town (particularly the Port area) and San Antonio, each of which provides a distinctive mood and environment.

4. Beaches and coastal beauty

More than 50 magnificent beaches and coves, each with its unique personality, can be found in Ibiza. Every preference may be satisfied by a beach, from busy and active beaches with beach clubs and water sports to calm coves with peaceful surroundings.

Some beaches are well-known for their stunning seascapes, while others are well known for their vibrant evening skies.

5. Historical and cultural landmarks

Learn more about the island's unique history by visiting the churches, forts, and other historical structures there. The old town of Ibiza (Dalt Vila), which is a UNESCO World Heritage site, is a maze of narrow cobblestone lanes and ancient defenses. Other notable cultural sites include Es Vedrà, a peculiar rock island, and Sa Caleta, a Phoenician hamlet.

6. Respect for the Environment

Ibiza has embraced ethical principles and sustainable tourism to protect its natural beauty. Visitors are asked to protect the environment, save water, and dispose of their trash properly. Several environmentally friendly initiatives and meetings are focused on protecting the island's natural environment.

7. Shopping and markets:

Ibiza offers a wide range of shopping options, from expensive shops in Ibiza Town to traditional markets and artisan businesses.

Find unique items, clothing, and crafts by exploring the hippie marketplaces in locations like Punta Arab and Las Dalias.

By being familiar with five essential aspects of Ibiza, you can make the most of your visit and fully take advantage of the range of offerings on the island. Regardless of whether you're searching for adventure, relaxation, or cultural immersion, Ibiza offers a fascinating and unique experience.

Essential Information for Visitors

Knowing important information as you prepare for your vacation to Ibiza helps ensure a trouble-free and enjoyable stay.

Your vacation to Ibiza will be enhanced if you are aware of these crucial elements, which include both practical guidance and safety considerations:

1. Currency & Payment:

The Euro (EUR) is the country's official unit of exchange, as it is across Spain. Although the vast majority of establishments accept credit cards, it's a good idea to have some extra cash on hand for minor purchases and establishments that may not accept cards.

2. Time Zone:

Ibiza observes Central European Time (CET) during the winter and Central European Summer Time (CEST) during the summer, with daylight saving time beginning in late March and ending in late October.

4. Emergency Number

Ibiza, like the rest of Spain, has an emergency number of 112. In the event of an emergency, dial this number to be connected to the police, ambulance, and fire departments.

5. Facilities for health and medicine:

Ibiza offers pharmacies and excellent medical services. You may go to the neighborhood health clinics (Centros de Salud) or the May Misses Hospital in Ibiza Town if you need medical care.

Make sure you have complete travel insurance that addresses any medical issues that may arise while you are away.

6. Safety precautions:

Ibiza is often a secure location for tourists. However, it's crucial to maintain vigilance and use common sense safety measures, such as protecting your possessions and paying attention to your surroundings, particularly in busy places.

7. Electricity:

Spain uses 230V as its standard voltage and 50Hz as its standard frequency. If your gadgets have different plug types than the European-style two-pin plugs (Type C and Type F) that are utilized, you may require a plug adaptor.

8. Internet and Connectivity

Hotels, cafés, and public areas all have plenty of Wi-Fi access. Additionally, several restaurants provide free Wi-Fi for visitors. Consider purchasing a local SIM card or an international data package from your cell provider if you want continual access.

9. Dress Code:

Ibiza offers a laid-back and informal vibe. Beachwear is OK for the beach and pool areas, however, while visiting cultural and religious sites or eating at luxury establishments, it is advised to dress modestly.

9. Water:

In Ibiza, drinking tap water is typically safe. Bottled water, which is commonly accessible at grocery stores and convenience stores, may, nevertheless, be preferred by certain guests.

10. Environmental Responsibility:

Ibiza lays a lot of focus on protecting the environment. To support the island's sustainability initiatives, be conscious of eco-friendly behaviors including lowering your use of plastic and recycling.

Budgeting For Your Ibiza Adventure

Setting a budget is an important part of arranging your vacation to Ibiza so that you can take advantage of everything the island has to offer without worrying about money. When planning your Ibiza vacation budget, take into account the following:

Accommodation:

Depending on the kind of hotel you choose and the time of year you visit, lodging fees might vary widely. Hostels and guesthouses provide more affordable alternatives, whereas luxury resorts and coastal hotels are often more costly.

Copyrighted Material

1. Transportation:

Your selected method of transportation will determine the cost of transportation. Budget for bus tickets or vehicle rental costs if you want greater freedom to explore the island if you intend to utilize public transportation.

2. Food and Dining

Depending on where you dine, dining expenses might change. Local cafes and tapas bars provide more economical alternatives, while upscale restaurants and beach clubs often have higher prices. Try the "menu del da" (menu of the day) while dining out; it often offers a decent bargain for a three-course meal.

3. Entertainment and Activities:

Spend money on the experiences and activities you want to have on your trip. Club dues, boat trips, water activities, and tourist excursions may fall under this category.

4. Nightlife:

The nightlife in Ibiza is a major magnet for tourists. Be prepared to pay for club admission fees, drinks, and other nightlife expenses since they may be expensive, particularly during the busiest times of the year.

5. Shopping and souvenirs:

Budget some money aside for souvenirs and shopping.

Ibiza's markets and boutique stores include one-of-a-kind goods and souvenirs to help you remember your stay.

6. All Other Expenses:

Include extra expenditures like gratuities, travel insurance, admission fees to attractions, and unforeseen charges.

Consider visiting during the shoulder seasons when lodging and activity costs may be lower to make the most of your money. Additionally, you may stretch your budget further by taking advantage of early bird savings on hotels and flights.

Copyrighted Material

How to get to Ibiza

Ibiza is easily accessible by several different modes of transportation, depending on where you are. The main ways to go to the alluring White Isle are as follows:

1. By Air:

The primary entry point to the island is Ibiza Airport (IBZ), which has excellent connections to several major international destinations in Europe. Regular flights by major airlines are offered to Ibiza from significant airports, especially during the busiest travel season. The length of your trip will depend on where you travel from, however many flights from European cities are just a few hours long.

2. From Ferry

You may take a ferry to Ibiza if you're already in Spain or one of the other Balearic Islands. Numerous ferry companies provide routes to the ports of Ibiza Town and San Antonio from towns including Barcelona, Valencia, Mallorca, and Formentera. An extremely beautiful way to access the island is via ferry, especially around sunset passages.

3. My boat or yacht:

Arriving in Ibiza by private yacht or charter boat is an alternative for individuals looking for an opulent and leisurely means of transportation. The marinas on the island provide a spectacular and special welcome experience for boats and sailors.

4. Using a Cruise Ship:

Some cruise companies include Ibiza in their Mediterranean itineraries during the busiest travel season. Passengers may spend the day exploring the island's activities and sights when cruise ships stop in Ibiza Town.

When you get to the island, you can get to Ibiza via buses, taxis, rental vehicles, and scooters. While cabs are easily accessible at taxi stands and in the main tourist destinations, public buses link major cities and attractions.

Renting a vehicle gives you the freedom to go to off-the-beaten-path locations and rural areas.

By choosing the most practical and appropriate form of transportation, you may anticipate an easy trip to Ibiza and start your discovery of this alluring Mediterranean jewel.

Best Time to Visit Ibiza

Ibiza's attractiveness is year-round, delivering a wide variety of experiences thanks to its magnetism that transcends seasons. Whether you're looking for a busy nightlife, picture-perfect beaches, or a more serene atmosphere, the ideal time to visit the island will depend on your interests. Here is a list of the many seasons and what they have to offer:

Copyrighted Material

From June until September, the summer

1. Ibiza's summer season is its busiest and draws tourists from all over the globe. The island comes to life during this season with a lively atmosphere, exciting nightlife, and several music festivals and events.

The Mediterranean Sea's waters are tempting for swimming and other water activities, and the beaches are sun-kissed. The island may be expected to have bright days, mild temperatures, and a buzzing atmosphere.

However, keep in mind that costs for lodging, food, and entertainment are often higher during this time of year and that crowds may form at popular locations.

Autumn (October) and Spring (April through May):

2. Ibiza is more serene and affordable during the shoulder seasons of spring and fall. Exploring the island's natural beauty and cultural sites is made possible by the good weather and warm temperatures.

Autumn offers stunning sunsets and a more relaxed mood, while spring adorns the island with blossoming flowers and verdant surroundings. The season for many beach clubs and other locations begins in May and ends in certain cases in October. You can take advantage of the island's attractions now without having to deal with the summertime throng.

November to March:

3. Ibiza is at its most serene during the winter, making it a great destination for anyone looking for a tranquil getaway and a window into local culture. While some clubs and tourist-oriented businesses shut during this time, many others—particularly in Ibiza Town—remain open.

You can still appreciate the island's natural beauty and cultural attractions because of the comparatively warm weather. Lower lodging costs and the opportunity to interact with locals and enjoy Ibiza's serene beauty are available throughout the winter months.

The ideal time to visit Ibiza ultimately depends on your choices and the kind of experience you're looking for. Ibiza offers something unique to offer all year long, whether you're seeking a buzzing nightlife, a relaxing beach vacation, or a cultural adventure.

Local Customs and Etiquette

Respecting Ibiza's culture by observing traditions and using proper etiquette is a great approach to improving your relationships with locals. Following are some vital traditions and etiquette pointers to bear in mind when you are there:

1. Greetings:

Warm handshakes or kisses on both cheeks are traditional ways for friends and acquaintances to greet each other when they first meet. When greeting individuals, say "Hola" (hello) and "Adiós" (goodbye). Good manners dictate that you say "Buenos das" (good morning) or "Buenas tardes" to the personnel when you enter a store or restaurant.

2. Clothing:

Despite the laid-back atmosphere in Ibiza, it is acceptable to dress modestly while visiting places of worship and cultural significance. Beachwear is allowed by the pool and on the beach, but while eating or strolling through town centers, cover up with proper attire.

3. Tipping:

In Spain, there is no need to tip since services are often included in the cost. But it's always nice to give a little more for really great service. If you're happy with the service, tip generously or round up the total.

4. Siesta:

Remember that many stores and businesses shut down for the customary siesta in the afternoon for a few hours. The speed of life slows down during this time, and it's typical to take a pause to rest or unwind.

5. Language:

Even though English is frequently spoken in tourist regions, the locals appreciate it when visitors make an effort to learn a few fundamental Spanish words. When expressing courtesy, a simple "gracias" or "por favor" goes a long way.

6. Photography:

When taking pictures, be mindful of other people's privacy, particularly in busy places or during cultural events. Always get permission before taking pictures of people, and be respectful of regional traditions.

7. Regard for the environment:

Ibiza is dedicated to ethical tourism and sustainability. By putting trash in the appropriate containers and using less plastic, you can demonstrate your concern for the environment. When visiting natural areas and beaches, particularly, be conscious of the delicate environment.

You will be welcomed into Ibiza's warm and welcoming culture by adhering to certain regional traditions and etiquette guidelines, making significant relationships with the people, and enhancing your trip experience.

CHAPTER 4 : LODGING AND ACCOMMODATIONS

Welcome to Ibiza

Welcome to the alluring island of Ibiza, where you can explore its sun-kissed beaches, exciting nightlife, and rich cultural history. Finding the ideal lodging before you go on your Ibiza vacation is crucial for a relaxing and enjoyable stay. The island has a broad selection of housing alternatives to fit different tastes and price ranges, including opulent beachfront resorts, quaint boutique hotels, and inexpensive hostels.

Here is a guide to assist you in selecting the best lodging for your stay in Ibiza:

1. Luxury Hotels and Resorts:

Ibiza offers an outstanding array of five-star hotels and luxury resorts for visitors looking for indulgence and leisure. These resorts often boast breathtaking coastal settings, opulent accommodations, top-notch facilities, and first-rate service. Private pools, spa services, fine restaurants, and breathtaking views of the Mediterranean Sea are all available. Ibiza's luxury resorts provide lavish and peaceful retreats to discriminating tourists.

2. Boutique lodging:

Ibiza is peppered with little boutique hotels that provide a fusion of design, personality, and attentive service.

These distinctive homes often include traditional Ibicenco architecture with a modern touch.

A memorable stay is made possible by the careful touches and unique experiences offered by boutique hotels.

3. Rural Retreats and Guesthouses:

Staying in guesthouses or rural getaways will allow you to experience Ibiza's true charm. These lodgings are often found outside of the busy tourist districts, providing a tranquil and complete immersion in the island's natural splendor. Enjoy the peace of the countryside as you are surrounded by beautiful scenery and historic buildings.

4.Guesthouses and Hostels at Low Prices:

Ibiza has several hostels and guesthouses that provide inexpensive and social housing choices for those on a tighter budget. Hostels are a popular option for backpackers and solitary explorers since they're a fantastic place to meet other travelers and swap tales. With so many affordable lodging options in the same area, visitors can easily reach the island's attractions and nightlife.

5. Renting apartments and villas:

If you want to feel at home even though you're not at home, think about renting an Ibiza apartment or villa. Families, groups of friends, or anyone in need of more room and privacy should choose this choice.

Apartment rentals and villas provide a cozy and practical base for your Ibiza adventure since they are furnished with kitchens, living rooms, and private outdoor areas.

Whatever kind of lodging you choose, be sure to reserve well in advance, particularly during the busiest times of the year, to guarantee your chosen choice. Finding and reserving the ideal accommodation in Ibiza is simple thanks to the abundance of hotels and other accommodations that provide online booking tools.

Arriving In Ibiza

Ibiza's welcoming Mediterranean atmosphere and the promise of an unforgettable voyage await you as you arrive on the island.

Here is a map that will help you go from the airport to the hotel of your choice so that your arrival will go as smoothly as possible:

1. Ibiza Airport (IBZ):

The primary international entry point to the island is Ibiza Airport, which is just 7.5 kilometers (4.7 miles) southwest of Ibiza Town. Numerous flights from significant European cities arrive at the airport often, particularly during the busiest travel period.

2. Transportation from the airport:

To get to your hotel after arriving, there are several different transit alternatives. These consist of:

- *Taxis:* Outside the airport building, taxis are easily accessible. For the majority of island destinations, there is a set charge for taxis that are regulated.
- *Buses:* An extensive network of public buses connects the Ibiza Airport to the island's main cities and tourist destinations. Tickets may be bought on the bus, which makes stops outside the arrivals area.
- *Rental Cars:* At the airport, you may find rental vehicle companies if you want the independence of touring the island at your leisure. you get the best deals, be sure you reserve your rental vehicle in advance.

- *Private Transfers:* To pick you up straight from the airport, several hotels and other lodgings provide private transport services. This choice is practical and guarantees a seamless transfer to your accommodation.

3. Getting Around the Island:

Several modes of transportation are available for traveling about the island after you've settled into your lodging.

Buses link major cities and tourist destinations and are a cheap and dependable form of public transportation. Additionally, taxis are often accessible, especially in metropolitan regions and popular tourist destinations.

Renting a vehicle or scooter enables you to see the island's most secluded and beautiful regions at your speed.

Language and Communication Tips

Although English is frequently spoken in tourist areas, Ibiza's official language is Spanish, making it reasonably simple to communicate with locals. However, adopting a few fundamental communication and language techniques can surely enhance your experience and encourage deep bonds with the islanders:

Basic Spanish Expressions

1. A few basic Spanish phrases can improve your communication and show that you are respectful of the community.

Consider learning how to say hello, use polite expressions, and say basic commands like asking for directions or placing an order.

Be Kind and Patient:

2. Be kind and patient while speaking with the natives. Most locals are kind and amiable and used to conversing with visitors. By saying "por favor" (please) and "gracias" (thank you) in your talks, you may demonstrate respect for regional traditions.

Tools and Apps for Languages:

3. During your travels, language applications and translation software might be useful tools. You may use these tools to quickly and easily browse discussions, understand options, and locate critical information.

Accept Local Customs

4. Embracing regional traditions and pleasantries, such as the Spanish habit of kissing strangers on both cheeks, demonstrates respect for the local culture. Asking for linguistic or cultural advice from the locals is never a bad idea; they will probably appreciate your interest in their culture.

Having conversations with hotel staff:

5. When dealing with hotel workers, don't be afraid to ask for help in English if you run across any language issues. Ibiza's hospitality sector is used to serving visitors from outside, so you can expect to get assistance from English-speaking workers.

Engage the Community:

6. Become a part of the community by interacting with and conversing with people to fully experience the culture. Going to festivals, going to local markets, and taking part in cultural activities may provide you with real-world experiences and opportunities to use your language abilities.

You'll discover that your interactions with the natives in Ibiza improve when you adopt these language and communication guidelines. Language constraints won't prevent you from forging lifelong friendships on this alluring Mediterranean island thanks to Ibiza's friendly and inviting culture.

Best Places to Stay In Ibiza

Making the most of your time on the island requires careful planning when booking your accommodations in Ibiza. Ibiza has a variety of areas, each with its distinct atmosphere and attractions. Here are some of the greatest locations to stay in Ibiza, regardless of whether you're looking for vibrant nightlife, pristine beaches, or peaceful countryside:

1. Town of Ibiza (Eivissa):

Ibiza Town, the island's capital and center of culture, provides the ideal fusion of excitement, modernism, and history. Stay in the historic center of Dalt Vila to experience the allure of medieval buildings, cobblestone streets, and breathtaking vistas from the old city walls. Ibiza Town is a bustling city with top-notch dining, shopping, and entertainment opportunities. The Marina Botafoch neighborhood, where there are upscale lodging options and hip beach clubs, is a favorite among celebrities.

2. The beach of the Bossa:

Playa d'en Bossa, which is south of Ibiza Town, is well known for its vibrant atmosphere and long, gorgeous sandy beach. This region is a popular destination for partygoers, featuring seaside clubs, pubs, and performances by well-known DJs. The busy nightlife scene is catered to by a variety of chic beachfront hotels and resorts in Playa d'en Bossa.

Town Of Ibiza(Eivissa)

Ibiza Beach

3. San Antoni de Portmany (San Antonio):

San Antonio, located on Ibiza's western coast, is renowned for its breathtaking sunsets and laid-back atmosphere. There are numerous pubs and cafes along the waterfront's Sunset Strip where you may take in the captivating nighttime views.

San Antonio provides a range of lodging choices, including inexpensive hostels and hotels with breathtaking views of the sun setting.

4. Saint Eulalia des Riu:

Consider vacationing in Santa Eulària des Riu on Ibiza's east coast for a more relaxed and welcoming atmosphere. This quaint village has a lovely marina, a lovely promenade, and a variety of eateries and stores. Santa Eulària des Riu is a great option for anyone looking for a peaceful getaway with quick access to the island's countryside and lovely beaches.

5. Ibiza's interior

Consider vacationing in the island's rural sections for a serene getaway surrounded by nature. A tranquil and true Ibicenco experience can be had in San Juan (Sant Joan de Labritja) and the central countryside. Agriturismo (farmhouses) and rustic guest houses let you experience the local way of life while letting you explore the island's natural splendor, secret coves, and beautiful hiking routes.

An Overview of Accommodation Options

Ibiza provides a wide range of lodging choices to suit the tastes and budgets of all visitors. The island features accommodations to suit all tastes, whether you're looking for opulence and pampering or something more cost-effective. An overview of the various lodging options in Ibiza is provided below:

1. Resorts and Hotels:

Ibiza is home to many hotels and resorts that can accommodate a variety of interests and styles. Private beach access, luxurious amenities, and fine cuisine are all features of luxury resorts. Boutique hotels offer cozy, fashionable lodging with individualized service.

Budget hotels offer reasonable options for guests looking for comfort without breaking the bank, while mid-range hotels offer cozy accommodations with useful features.

2. Guesthouses and Hostels:

Budget-conscious visitors and lone adventurers frequently choose hostels and guesthouses. These lodging options provide individual or shared dorm rooms, as well as common areas for meeting other tourists. Hostels are perfect for individuals looking to meet new people and enjoy the island together because they frequently arrange group activities.

3. Condos and villas:

For families, parties, or tourists who value solitude and space, apartment rentals and villas provide a home-away-from-home experience. These lodgings have kitchens and living rooms, giving guests the freedom to make meals and spend downtime in a relaxing environment.

4. Rural retreats and agriturismos:

Consider staying in agriturismo (farmhouses) or rural getaways for a distinctive and all-encompassing experience of Ibiza's countryside. With the island's natural beauty and agricultural landscapes all around them, these hotels offer a genuine and peaceful retreat.

5. Green lodgings and glamping:

Ibiza provides eco-lodges and glamping locations for guests who value sustainability and a distinctive holiday experience.

Enjoy a closer relationship with nature while reducing your influence on the environment.

6. Stays on yachts and boats:

Consider staying on a yacht or charter boat for a lavish and unique experience. The marinas in Ibiza provide a variety of yachts and boats with roomy rooms and the chance to explore the island's coastline and neighboring bays.

Whatever kind of lodging you select, make sure to reserve early, especially during the busiest times of the year, to guarantee your chosen choice. Your vacation on the White Isle will be relaxing, enjoyable, and catered to your preferences thanks to the variety of tastes and interests catered to by Ibiza's hotels.

CHAPTER 5 : **NAVIGATING IBIZA**

Getting Around the Island

Thanks to the island's well-developed transportation system, getting around is a breeze. The island provides a variety of practical means of transportation, enabling you to easily visit its several areas, attractive villages, and breathtaking beaches. Here is a detailed map that will help you navigate Ibiza:

1. Commuter Buses:

The public buses in Ibiza connect the main towns and tourist attractions, offering a cheap and dependable form of transportation.

The bus service runs often and provides air-conditioned comfort for passengers, especially during the busiest travel season. Ibiza Town serves as the primary bus terminal, and routes connect there with Santa Eulària des Riu, San Antonio, and other important locations.

2. Taxis:

Taxis are easily accessible all around the island and provide a practical means to get between towns and well-known destinations. You can either find taxis at marked taxi ranks or flag one down on the street. Taxi fares are metered, and most of the island's attractions are known to the drivers.

3. Scooters and rental cars:

Renting a vehicle allows you to explore Ibiza at your leisure and find places that are off the main path. The airport and major cities each have a large number of automobile rental companies. Keep in mind that it's best to reserve your rental car ahead of time during the busy season. Travelers seeking a thrilling and quick way to get about the island frequently rent scooters.

4. Biking:

Ibiza is biker-friendly since it has bike lanes and picturesque paths. Consider renting a bike to tour the island's rural and coastal districts if you enjoy cycling. Bicycles are frequently available for rent at hotels.

5. Ferries and Water Taxis:

A pleasant and picturesque method to get between coastal cities and adjacent islands is by taking a water taxi or ferry. Ferries connect Ibiza with the nearby island of Formentera, allowing for a lovely day trip. Additionally, there are water taxis that provide transportation between well-known beach clubs and coastal locations.

6. Private excursions and tours:

Consider scheduling private tours and excursions to visit particular locations of interest for a hassle-free experience. You can explore Ibiza's natural beauty and cultural richness on boat rides, sightseeing tours, and other adventurous activities with the help of knowledgeable local guides.

7. Walking Around:

Ibiza is perfect for exploring on foot because of its small size and lovely streets. Walk through Dalt Vila's winding streets, wander along the seaside promenades, and enjoy the stunning coastline vistas.

You have a wide range of transportation alternatives at your disposal, making moving about Ibiza easy and fun. Whether you like the independence of driving your car or the carefree atmosphere of public transportation, each means of transportation ensures a special trip on the alluring White Isle.

Islands Of Ibiza

Copyrighted Material

The Top Places to Visit in Ibiza

Ibiza is an island full of undiscovered treasures, each with its special charm and intrigue. As you begin your journey, be sure to stop by these prominent locations, which highlight the island's varied landscapes, vibrant culture, and extensive history:

1. Ibiza Town's Dalt Vila

Dalt Vila, Ibiza's ancient old town, is a UNESCO World Heritage site and a must-see location. This lovely tangle of cobblestone alleyways, charming plazas, and historical landmarks gives panoramic views of the Mediterranean Sea while being enclosed within medieval fortifications.

To learn more about the intriguing history of the island, visit the Cathedral of SantaMara, the Almudaina Castle, and the Archaeological Museum.

2. The Es Vedrà

This mysterious rock island off the coast of Ibiza is a mesmerizing sight and the source of several stories and legends. Es Vedrà is a naturally protected location, and the best places to observe it are from vantage points along the coast, like Cala d'Hort. It is a mesmerizing sight to see its magnificent silhouette against the setting sun.

6. Nevada City:

Las Salinas, a lovely nature reserve south of Ibiza, is well-known for its salt flats and immaculate beaches.

One of the island's most well-liked beaches, Playa de Ses Salines is renowned for its pristine waters and exciting beach clubs. Along with the famous salt pans, the reserve is home to a variety of bird species.

7. **Saint Eulalia des Riu**:

Santa Eulària des Riu is a picturesque community with a laid-back vibe on the east coast. Take strolls along the seafront by the sea, tour the Puig de Missa hilltop church, and browse the Hippy Market for one-of-a-kind keepsakes.

The harbor at Santa Eulària des Riu is a lovely place to eat while taking in the scenery.

CALLA COMETE

This beautiful west coast beach is well-known for its azure waters and captivating sunsets. Cala Comte (Cala Conta), which is divided among several coves, provides beautiful locations for swimming, snorkeling, and sunbathing.

Formentera:

Despite not being a part of Ibiza, the neighboring island of Formentera is only accessible by ferry and is a fantastic day excursion. Formentera is a haven for nature lovers and beach lovers with its immaculate beaches, clean waters, and relaxed environment.

Bay of San Antonio:

San Antonio Bay offers an exciting nightlife scene and an amazing location to view the sunset. The Sunset Strip is a well-known location for taking in the nighttime show while sipping cocktails at venerable establishments like Café del Mar and Mambo.

Hippy Market and Es Canar:

Punta Arab, the original hippie market, is located in Es Canar, a city on the east coast of the island. The market comes alive every Wednesday with a diverse assortment of arts, crafts, apparel, and live music, providing a distinctive shopping and cultural experience.

You may experience Ibiza's vibrant culture and rich natural beauty as you travel to these popular locations. A tour into the heart of the Mediterranean is sure to be enjoyable and interesting because each location has its attraction and tales to tell.

Exploring the Beautiful Beaches

The beaches of Ibiza are the definition of paradise with their clean waters, soft sands, and breathtaking surroundings. The island offers a wide variety of beaches to fit your preferences, whether you're looking for lively beach clubs, quiet coves, or family-friendly coasts.

Here are a few of Ibiza's most stunning beaches to visit:

1. The beach of the Bossa:

A popular destination for partygoers, this long, active beach offers a bustling atmosphere with beachfront bars and clubs. The lively atmosphere, variety of water activities, and beachside sunbeds and loungers make Playa d'en Bossa popular.

2. Cala Comte (Cala Conta)

The turquoise waters and spectacular sunset views at Cala Comte are well known. The beach is separated into several coves, each with its allure. Swimming, snorkeling, and sunbathing are all great activities at this well-liked location.

4. Jondal, Cala:

Cala Jondal, a fashionable beach on the island's south coast, is well-known for its posh beach clubs and celebrity sightings. Enjoy eating delicious food at the beachside eateries while relaxing on plush daybeds.

5. Cala Salada as well as Cala Saladeta:

These adjacent coves are some of Ibiza's most beautiful and remote beaches. Cala Salada and Cala Saladeta, which are surrounded by cliffs covered with pine trees, have clean waters and a peaceful atmosphere that are ideal for snorkeling and relaxation.

6. Playa de Ses Salines, Ses Salines:

Ses Salines is a beautiful beach with golden beaches and calm seas that is located within a nature preserve. This well-known location features coastal eateries and pubs and draws a diverse audience.

7. Cala Vadella

Cala Vadella is a tranquil beach that is ideal for swimming and water sports because it is family-friendly. Hills surround the shore, creating a secluded and private environment.

8. Xarraca, Cala:

On the island's northern coast, go to Cala Xarraca for a more untouched and natural experience.

The reddish cliffs, crystal-clear water, and medicinal mud baths in this cove are its most notable features.
azure waters

Aguas Blancas is a dreamy beach encircled by cliffs and rich flora, nestled in a lovely harbor.
The beach draws nature enthusiasts and anyone looking for a tranquil escape because of its pristine beauty and nudist-friendly area.

Remember to preserve the environment by engaging in responsible tourism while you visit Ibiza's breathtaking beaches.

Since many of these beaches are located within protected zones, it's important to abide by the rules and leave no evidence of your presence.

In this Mediterranean paradise, Ibiza's beaches provide the ideal backdrop for making lifelong memories, whether you're looking for adventure, leisure, or socializing.

Exciting Tours And Activities: Boat Trips

When visiting Ibiza, you must explore the island's beautiful shoreline and blue ocean. Boat tours are one of the most thrilling ways to take in the splendor of the Mediterranean.

There is a boat tour to suit every choice, whether you want to travel to secluded coves, explore nearby islands, or have a good time on the open sea. Here are a few exciting boat trips you can take in Ibiza:

1. Take a boat tour that allows you to travel between the nearby islands of Formentera and Ibiza. Discover the pristine beaches, crystal-clear waters, and relaxed atmosphere of Formentera.
2. Numerous boat cruises feature stops where passengers can go swimming or snorkeling in the clear seas.
3. Sunset Cruises: Take a sunset cruise to see the renowned Ibiza sunset from the water.

As the sun sinks below the horizon, observe as you sail along the coast how the sky is painted in shades of orange and pink. These cruises frequently feature cocktails, live music, and a mystical ambiance.

4. Join a boat tour to visit secluded coves and caverns that are inaccessible from the ground. Explore destinations like Atlantis, Es Vedrà, and Cala d'en Serra to see their breathtaking rock formations and clean seas.

5. Party Boats: Party boats are a well-liked option for people looking for an exciting and colorful experience. As you cruise around the coast with like-minded partygoers, dance to the newest sounds, have cocktails, and soak up the sun.

6. Discover the colorful marine life that resides beneath the waves of Ibiza on a snorkeling adventure. Numerous boat cruises offer snorkeling gear and instruction, enabling you to see the beauties of the ocean floor.

7. Private Yacht Charters: Treat yourself to privacy and luxury by hiring a private yacht. Create an itinerary that suits your preferences, whether you want a romantic cruise, a party with friends, or a day of relaxation and watersports.

8. Join eco-friendly boat tours that emphasize marine conservation and seeing local species, like dolphins and sea birds. Marine species Tours. These excursions offer opportunities to learn about the island's fragile nature.

Select boat captains who are reputable, licensed, and have an emphasis on sustainability and safety.

There are a variety of boat tours available in Ibiza, so no matter whether you want a peaceful cruise or a wild party, a boat excursion will satisfy your preferences.

Rural Hotels and Rustic Retreats

Ibiza's rural hotels and rustic getaways offer a calm and genuine vacation experience. These lodgings provide a special chance to experience the island's natural beauty and way of life firsthand.

Here's a closer look at the attractiveness and charm of Ibiza's rural accommodations:

1. Farmhouses (Agroturismos):

Traditional farms that have been turned into attractive lodgings are called agriturismos. These homes frequently have tranquil gardens, rustic furnishings, and working farms where you can see old-fashioned farming techniques in action.

You may escape the rush of city life at an agriturismo by enjoying a tranquil and immersive experience.

2. Countryside Hotels :

Ibiza's rural hotels offer a seamless fusion of contemporary comfort and pastoral charm.

These hotels offer a tranquil retreat with breathtaking views of the countryside as they are tucked away in the island's gorgeous settings. Take use of facilities like gardens, swimming pools, and regional cuisine produced with seasonal ingredients from nearby farmers.

3. Glamping and Eco-Lodge Locations:

Ibiza has eco-lodges and glamping locations that blend comfort and sustainability for tourists that care about the environment.

These eco-friendly lodgings employ renewable energy, encourage ethical travel, and provide distinctive stays in tune with the environment. While camping in opulent tents, you may appreciate nature without giving up modern luxuries.

4. Wellness Retreats:

Numerous wellness resorts with a focus on rest, renewal, and holistic experiences may be found in rural Ibiza. Participate in yoga and meditation classes, treat yourself to spa services, and enjoy wholesome food produced with regional ingredients.

5. Artistic Retreats:

Ibiza has a few rural lodging options for creative types looking for privacy and inspiration. These retreats offer tranquil locations that foster creativity and give a tranquil backdrop for introspection.

A distinctive approach to exploring the peaceful side of Ibiza and connecting with the island's natural beauty is to stay in rural hotels and rustic retreats.

Rural lodging options in Ibiza provide a glimpse of real island life, whether you're looking for leisure, cultural immersion, or an eco-friendly getaway.

Sampling the Local Culinary Delights

The cuisine of Ibiza is a beautiful combination of cosmopolitan flavors, fresh local ingredients, and Mediterranean tastes. Your trip to Ibiza must include exploring the island's culinary delights.

Here are some Ibiza eating options and culinary treats you simply must try:

Traditional Ibicenco dishes

Try some of the authentic Ibicenco dishes that represent the island's gastronomic heritage.

Try "Bullit de Peix," a traditional fish stew prepared with saffron, potatoes, and locally caught fish. Another well-known dish is called "Sofrit Pagès" and it consists of lamb, poultry, and potatoes that have been cooked with garlic and herbs.

Fish and fresh seafood:

Ibiza is a famous island known for its seafood and fish delicacies. Enjoy "Gambas Rojas" (red prawns), "Calamari a la

Plancha" (grilled squid), and "Suquet de Peix" (fish stew) that have been grilled. "Parrilladas de Pescado," or mixed seafood barbecues, are common in restaurants.

Coastal Chiringuitos:

Enjoy the laid-back atmosphere at the seaside "chiringuitos" (beach bars).

With the sand beneath your feet and views of the ocean, these relaxed restaurants provide fresh seafood, paella, and regional cuisine.

"Hierbas" liqueur from Ibiza:

Try some "Hierbas Ibicencas," the island's traditional herbal liqueur, to go with your meals.

It's often served as a digestif after meals and is made from a combination of regional herbs and spices.

Hippie markets and regional food:

Visit the vibrant hippy markets on the island, such as Las Dalias in San Carlos and Punta Arab in Es Canar. These markets provide a wide range of regional goods, including artisanal cheeses, olive oil, honey, and handcrafted goods.

International and fusion cuisine:

The eating scene in Ibiza also offers a variety of fusion foods and modern cuisines to suit different culinary preferences. Enjoy imaginative culinary creations that blend regional ingredients with influences from around the world.

Experiments in Fine Dining:

Treat yourself to a gourmet dining experience at one of the island's finest restaurants on a special occasion. A lot of these places have Michelin stars and serve fine dining with expensive wines.

Paella, a traditional rice dish from Spain, and "fideuà," a dish similar to paella but cooked with short pasta, are two dishes you must taste while visiting Ibiza. Though there are meat and vegetarian options, both are often made with seafood.

Ibiza's cuisine is diverse, so when you eat there, take your time to savor the flavors, take in the laid-back atmosphere, and appreciate it. Ibiza's food culture offers a fantastic voyage for your taste senses, with everything from casual cafes to fine dining establishments.

CHAPTER 6 : EXPERIENCING IBIZA'S NIGHTLIFE AND ENTERTAINMENT

The nightlife and entertainment scene in Ibiza is legendary and attracts revelers and music fans from all over the world. The island provides an amazing variety of experiences that appeal to every taste, from world-class clubs to historic gems. With the following chapters, you may fully experience Ibiza's dynamic nightlife and learn about its unexplored historical gems:

Dinning and Gastronomic Experiences

Ibiza's gastronomic journey goes beyond regional specialties; the island also has a vibrant eating scene that welcomes foodies from all walks of life.

Ibiza offers a great culinary experience that tempts the taste buds, with options ranging from upscale dining establishments to beachfront chiringuitos. Here are some dining opportunities you shouldn't pass up:

- Beachfront Chiringuitos : Indulge in a casual dining experience at one of Ibiza's chiringuitos on the beach. Enjoy paella, tapas, and seafood that have just been caught while gazing out at the ocean and feeling the sand under your toes.

- Enjoy the farm-to-table cuisine that so many of Ibiza's restaurants are embracing. Enjoy food prepared with organic fruit, artisanal cheeses, an free-range meats that are all produced locally.

- Fusion Food: Ibiza's culinary scene embraces fusion food, which combines regional flavors with influences from around the world. Discover innovative recipes that showcase the island's innovative and diverse cuisine.
- Restaurants with Michelin Stars: Indulge in a fine dining experience at one of Ibiza's restaurants with a Michelin star. In a sumptuous atmosphere, indulge in exceptional gourmet cuisine coupled with specially selected wines.
- Dining al fresco while taking in one of Ibiza's famous sunsets.

A wonderful atmosphere is created for an exceptional dining experience at many of the restaurants along the coast that offer breathtaking sunset views.

- Ibiza's "Hierbas" Liqueur is the ideal way to round off a culinary voyage. After your dinner, have a taste of this traditional herbal liqueur, which honors the island's herbal heritage: "Hierbas Ibicencas."

The Best Clubs for Nightlife Enthusiasm

The nightlife in Ibiza is known for its prestigious clubs, which have played host to some of the biggest DJs and electronic music festivals in the world. At these renowned locations, get ready to dance the night away:

1. Amnesia is a must-visit club for fans of dance music because of its renowned parties and wide range of musical selections.

   The Main Room and the Club Room, the club's two rooms, offer a variety of electronic music experiences.

2. Pacha: A landmark of Ibiza's nightlife, Pacha has been providing crowd-pleasing entertainment for years. Pacha is still a must-visit location on any Ibiza party itinerary thanks to its chic decor, upbeat ambiance, and top-notch DJs.

3. Ushuaa: A refuge for daytime revelers, Ushuaa offers a distinctive open-air experience with top-tier DJs spinning by the pool.

An amazing party environment is created by the fusion of music, entertainment, and bright energy.

4. DC-10: Well-known for its underground electronic music scene, DC-10 draws ardent followers of techno and house music. After-hours activities at the club are very renowned and popular.

5. H Ibiza: With cutting-edge sound systems and a stellar roster of international DJs, H Ibiza keeps making waves in the partying industry. The immersive sights and modern design improve the party atmosphere.

6. Heart Ibiza is an avant-garde idea that fuses food, art, and music for a holistic experience. Enjoy performances by well-known performers while indulging in Michelin-starred chefs' gourmet masterpieces.

7. Privilege: One of the biggest clubs in the world with a legendary superclub status and awe-inspiring ambiance, Privilege promises an amazing dance celebration.

As many of Ibiza's clubs organize special events and parties throughout the week, be sure to schedule your clubbing evenings in advance. No matter, if you prefer techno, house, or electronic dance music, Ibiza's nightlife, will leave you with priceless memories of dancing under the sky.

Unearthing Historic Gems

Ibiza is home to several historical treasures that highlight its rich cultural history and historic past in addition to its thriving nightlife. Discover the fascinating history of the island by exploring its historical sites:

1. Dalt Vila: Start your tour by taking a stroll around Dalt Vila, the center of Ibiza Town. The Cathedral of Santa Mara, the Almudaina Castle, and the historic city walls are just a few of the historical sites in this UNESCO-designated old town. Explore its cobblestone streets while taking in the fascinating history and breathtaking views.

2. Find out about the ancient Phoenician community of Sa Caleta, which dates

to the seventh century BCE. This archeological site provides a window into the lifestyle of the island's first settlers.

3. Visit Puig de Missa, a fortified church that overlooks the town, in the charming hilltop village of Santa Eulària des Riu. Discover the religious and cultural significance of the area by exploring the church and its museum.

4. Es Canar Hippy Market: At the Es Canar Hippy Market, you may learn more about Ibiza's colorful past. This market, which was established in the 1970s, is a wonderful place to find one-of-a-kind gifts and crafts while showcasing the island's counter-cultural background.

5. Explore Ibiza's prehistoric past at the Necropolis del Puig des Molins, a sizable burial site that dates back to the Phoenician-Punic period. The location has a large number of burial chambers and antiquated objects, which shed light on the island's funerary customs.

6. Sant Rafel: Take a stroll around the quaint village of Sant Rafel, which is renowned for its whitewashed homes and old church. This village provides a tranquil setting and a chance to learn about the indigenous Ibicenco way of life.

7. Can Marçà Caves: Visit Puerto de San Miguel's interesting Can Marçà Caves.

The guided tour reveals the history of the caverns as a smuggler's haven as it leads you past breathtaking stalactites, subterranean lakes, and secret chambers.

Discovering Ibiza's historical treasures will help you understand the island's rich cultural history and its significance throughout the ages. Ibiza's historical assets, which range from ancient ruins to quaint villages, deepen the island's attraction.

Enjoying The Quaint Bars

Ibiza is known for its vibrant clubs, but the island also has tiny bars that provide a more laid-back and private aspect of nightlife.

These lovely businesses offer a distinctive environment that is ideal for socializing with friends, getting to know locals, and having a more relaxed evening. Here are some of the best locations in Ibiza to take in the charming bar scene:

1. Bar Anita (San Carlos): Since the 1950s, this historic bar has served as a meeting spot for locals and tourists alike in the little community of San Carlos.

This rustic pub is well-known for its "hierbas" liquor, traditional tapas, and bohemian atmosphere. It exudes a nostalgic appeal.

2. Santa Gertrudis' (Can Tixedó Art Café) is a nice place to enjoy coffee, beverages, and live music. It is located right in the center of Santa Gertrudis. The pub has a gallery and frequently hosts performances by regional musicians and artists.

3. Santa Eulària des Riu's Kiosko S'Embarcador is a kiosk bar with spectacular sea views and a laid-back ambiance. It is situated beside the marina. It's the perfect place to unwind while enjoying a cool beverage and watching the boats go by.

4. Although known for its hippy market, Las Dalias (San Carlos) also has a bustling pub with a bohemian atmosphere.

Drinks, live music, and dancing under the stars are all available in the lovely garden environment.

5. Can Jordi Blues Station (San José): This blues-themed pub features live jazz and blues performances, resulting in a genuine and soulful atmosphere. It's a terrific location to listen to quality music and meet other music lovers.

6. Chirincana (Es Cavallet Beach): Chirincana is a beach bar with a laid-back atmosphere that is located on Es Cavallet Beach. Sit back and unwind on the plush lounge beds while enjoying cocktails, delectable meals, and stunning sunsets.

7. Cala Conta's Sunset Ashram is the ideal location to view Ibiza's renowned sunsets, as its name suggests.

Ibiza for Families: Enjoyable for Everyone

Ibiza is not just a party island; it also offers family-friendly activities and attractions that are appropriate for all ages. If you're traveling with kids, take into account these family-friendly activities:

1. Beach Days: Ibiza has many beaches that are suitable for families and have shallow waters, making it safe for kids to play and swim there.

Family-friendly beaches in the area include Talamanca, Playa d'en Bossa, and Cala Llonga.

2. Spend the day in one of Ibiza's aquatic parks, such as Sirenis Aquagames Water Park or Aguamar Water Park. The entire family will enjoy the water slides, swimming areas, and other water activities at these parks.

3. Cova de Can Marçà: Visit the Cova de Can Marçà caverns in Puerto de San Miguel on a family-friendly trip. The guided tour of the caves includes an engrossing narrative, making it an exciting and instructive trip for kids.

4. Enjoy a horseback riding adventure in the lovely landscape of Ibiza.

Numerous equestrian facilities provide guided trips appropriate for riders of any skill level.

5. Acrobosc Ibiza is an adventure park with ziplines, rope courses, and other outdoor activities ideal for both kids and adults. It is situated in Santa Eulària des Riu.

6. Hippy Market Es Canar: Shop at the family-friendly Es Canar Hippy Market for handicrafts, clothing, and toys to keep the kids occupied.

7. Discover Ibiza's lovely villages, including Santa Gertrudis and Sant Rafel, which provide a laid-back environment and family-friendly restaurants.

Embracing Sustainable Tourism Practices

Adopting sustainable tourism practices is essential to maintaining Ibiza's natural beauty and cultural history as the island draws more tourists every year. Here are some ideas about how to travel responsibly and sustainably in Ibiza:

1. Support Local Businesses: To help the community's economy, choose to eat at home-grown eateries, shop at independent boutiques, and stay in eco-friendly lodgings.

2. Reduce Plastic Use: Use reusable water bottles, shopping bags, and straws instead of single-use plastics. Ibiza has many businesses that are dedicated to minimizing plastic waste.

Copyrighted Material

3. Respect the Environment: When visiting natural places, stay on the routes that have been set out, don't bother the wildlife, and don't leave any rubbish behind.

4. Conserve Water: Because of the island's reputation for arid weather, water should be used sparingly.

5. Use Public Transportation: To lessen your carbon impact while exploring the island, think about taking the public bus or cycling.

6. Participate in Sustainable Activities: Pick tours and excursions that put a focus on sustainability and encourage ethical travel.

Copyrighted Material

7. Learn about the Culture: To better comprehend and appreciate Ibiza's distinctive legacy, immerse yourself in the island's history and culture.

Adopting sustainable tourism practices will help you protect Ibiza's beauty for future generations and will benefit the environment and local community.

Copyrighted Material

CHAPTER 7 : **OUTDOOR ADVENTURES IN IBIZA**

Beautiful scenery and a variety of terrain in Ibiza offer thrill-seekers and nature lovers a variety of outdoor excursions. The island offers something for everyone to appreciate the grandeur of its natural beauties, from thrilling pursuits to peaceful retreats. We shall examine the outdoor pursuits and undiscovered attractions in Ibiza in this chapter

Engaging In Outdoor Activities

Ibiza's breathtaking natural beauty provides the backdrop for a variety of outdoor pursuits that let you discover and interact with the island's landscape. The best outdoor activities in Ibiza are listed below:

Copyrighted Material

1. Nature paths and Hiking: Lace up your hiking boots and head out on one of the many beautiful nature paths that wind through pine forests, seaside cliffs, and rural areas. As you travel the island's varied geography, find undiscovered coves, historic sites, and breathtaking perspectives.

2. Cycling Tours: Discover Ibiza on two wheels with cycling tours that are appropriate for cyclists of all skill levels. Cycling offers a terrific opportunity to see the island's natural beauty, from relaxing rides along coastal paths to strenuous mountain bike tracks.

3. Stand-Up Paddleboarding (SUP): On a stand-up paddleboard, take in the

peace of Ibiza's crystal-clear waters. Explore sea caves and undiscovered beaches as you float down the coast, taking in the breathtaking scenery and abundant marine life.

4. Kayaking: Take a kayaking journey along Ibiza's shoreline. As you go across the island's crystal-clear seas, you will come across isolated coves, striking cliffs, and marine sanctuaries.

5. Cliff leaping: Ibiza provides opportunities for cliff leaping into the abysmal, blue water for thrill-seekers. A safe jumping location may be found with the help of knowledgeable guides, so you can experience the rush of adrenaline while surrounded by the beauty of nature.

6. Scuba diving and snorkeling: Explore the diverse marine life of Ibiza's underwater paradise. Explore underwater caverns and shipwrecks by scuba diving or snorkeling in shallow seas to see colorful fish and marine life.

7. Riding a horse is a peaceful way to explore the countryside of Ibiza. Take advantage of guided tours that give you a special view of the island's natural splendor as they lead you through olive groves, pine forests, and rural pathways.

8. Rock Climbing: Ibiza has cliffs and breathtaking sea vistas for rock climbers. Experienced climbers can have a gratifying and exciting

experience scaling the island's limestone cliffs.

Discovering Hidden Gems and Secret Spots

Ibiza is decorated with hidden treasures and secret locations that reward travelers willing to veer off the beaten road in addition to the island's well-known attractions. These less well-known areas provide a sense of seclusion and an opportunity to develop a closer relationship with nature. Some of Ibiza's untapped hidden gems are listed below:

1. Atlantis (Sa Pedrera) is a disused quarry with unusual rock formations that are tucked away in a quiet cove close to Cala d'Hort.

2. Locals and tourists seeking a mysterious and quiet experience love this hidden location.
3. Views of Es Vedrà: There are various secret locations where you may enjoy the best views of this famous rock island off the west coast of Ibiza. Views of the beautiful island and the glistening Mediterranean Sea are breathtaking from these vantage points.
4. Visit Cala Xuclar, a tranquil and less popular beach on the northern shore, to get away from the throng.

This undiscovered treasure offers calm surroundings and clean waters that are ideal for snorkeling and relaxation.

5. Locals love Punta Galera, a secluded rocky cove close to San Antonio, for its pristine seas and unmanicured granite terraces that are perfect for sunbathing and taking in the breathtaking sunset.

6. Ses Fontanelles is a significant archaeological site with centuries-old sculptures that offer an insight into Ibiza's prehistoric past. Explore the stunning rock engravings at Ses Fontanelles.

7. Sa Talaia: Hike to the top of Sa Talaia, Ibiza's highest point, for stunning panoramic views of the entire island. Hikers can enjoy breathtaking views of the nearby countryside and shoreline on this less popular track.

8. Drumming at Benirràs Beach: On Sundays, go to Benirràs Beach to take in a distinctive Ibiza custom of drumming at dusk. Locals and guests join together for a spectacular evening of music and community at this energetic and spiritual gathering.

9. The Es Cubells viewpoint, tucked away in Ibiza's southwest, provides uninterrupted views of the Mediterranean Sea and the adjacent island of Formentera.

Discovering these hidden locations will take you to peaceful and awe-inspiring moments where you can appreciate Ibiza's extraordinary natural beauty and attractiveness.

CHAPTER 8 : EXPLORING IBIZA'S NATURAL BEAUTY

Ibiza's natural beauty is a mesmerizing tapestry of spectacular vistas, charming communities, and gorgeous sunsets. This chapter will provide a deeper understanding of Ibiza's varied natural attractions by delving into the island's captivating landscape and little settlements.

Chasing Stunning Sunsets

Ibiza is well known for its mesmerizing sunsets, which paint the sky with a kaleidoscope of hues as the sun sets. Visitors and residents alike are drawn to the island's spectacular evening splendor by these enchanting moments, which provide a sense of calm and awe.

The following locations in Ibiza are some of the best for catching gorgeous sunsets:

1. One of the most well-known places to view the sunset in Ibiza is the Sunset Strip in San Antonio. It offers a lively environment as the sun sets over the water, accompanied by live music and drumming, and is lined with bustling clubs and restaurants.

2. Es Vedrà: Visit the southwestern coast to take in the breathtaking sunset views of this mysterious rock island that rises out of the water. The sun setting behind this fabled monument is spectacular from the Cala d'Hort viewpoint.

3. Benirràs Beach is well-known for its Sunday evening drumming sessions, where drummers come together to create a special and rhythmic atmosphere as the sun sets on the day.

4. On the western shore of the island, near Cala Comte (Cala Conta), visitors may enjoy breathtaking sunset views over the glistening Mediterranean Sea. The stunning shoreline and beautiful oceans only serve to enhance the charm of watching the sunset.

5. Punta Galera: A secret paradise for those who love to watch the sunset over the calm sea, Punta Galera provides natural rock terraces perfect for sunset picnics and quiet introspection.

6. Portinatx Lighthouse: Located on Ibiza's northern shore, the Portinatx Lighthouse offers a beautiful backdrop for watching the sunset.

It provides sweeping views of the beach and the setting sun because it is perched on a cliff.

7. Cala Salada: Take in the magnificent sunset from the charming Cala Salada beach, where the serene surroundings create a cozy and beautiful mood.

8. Santa Eulària des Riu: A wonderful place to watch the sunset while wandering along the shore is the promenade at Santa Eulària des Riu.

Each of these spots gives a distinctive view of Ibiza's natural beauty as the sun sets over the horizon, making sunset chasing a cherished tradition on the island.

Visiting Picturesque Villages

Ibiza is filled with lovely villages that radiate genuine charm and a sense of tranquility outside of the busy tourist centers. You may engage with island culture and learn about the slower-paced, traditional Ibicenco way of life by exploring these charming hamlets.

Here are a few of Ibiza's lovely communities that you simply must visit:

Copyrighted Material

1. Santa Gertrudis is a little settlement in the middle of the island that is well-known for its artistic community and bohemian atmosphere. Enjoy the shade of its lovely center square, which is home to several cafes, shops, and art galleries.

2. Sant Joan de Labritja is a town on Spain's northern coast that is encircled by verdant scenery and quaint traditional homes. Visit the village church and take a tour of the beautiful shoreline and rolling hills around.

3. Sant Carles de Peralta: Sant Carles de Peralta, renowned for its laid-back

atmosphere and hippy tradition, is the perfect place to embrace the true Ibicenco attitude. The craft markets and studios in this village serve as a showcase for regional ingenuity.

4. Sant Rafel: Offering a scenic environment, Sant Rafel is surrounded by almond and olive groves.

A lovely whitewashed church and several quaint cafes and eateries can be found throughout the area.

5. Es Cubells: Es Cubells offers sweeping views of the ocean and Formentera from its perch atop a cliff on the southwest coast.

This serene community is perfect for discovering secret coves and taking in the calm of the countryside.

6. Sant Josep de sa Talaia is a charming place to explore with its typical white buildings and winding streets. Several of Ibiza's breathtaking beaches and coves can be reached from the village.

7. Puig d'en Valls: With its traditional architecture and small-town atmosphere, Puig d'en Valls, which is near Ibiza Town, provides glimpse of local life.

8. Jess: Located not far from Ibiza Town, Jess combines historic charm with contemporary conveniences. It's an easy place to explore because of its proximity to the capital.

It is possible to get a sense of Ibiza's true character when strolling through these charming villages, mingling with the inhabitants, and taking in the island's rich history.

Unveiling The Regions Of Ibiza

Ibiza is a tapestry of distinct locations, each with its attraction and personality; it is not simply one single travel destination. The island's regions offer unique experiences for visitors to relish, ranging from colorful seaside sceneries to tranquil rural settings. The various regions of Ibiza will be uncovered in this section, along with information on their charms and attractions.

1. Ibiza Town (Eivissa): Ibiza Town, or Eivissa in Catalan, is the island's capital and its energetic, cultural center. With its age-old fortification walls and picturesque cobblestone walkways, the historic Dalt Vila, a UNESCO World Heritage site, dominates the skyline.

By visiting the cathedral, museums, and galleries in this location, you may completely immerse yourself in history. The modern marina, where hip eateries, bars, and boutiques foster a cosmopolitan ambiance, shares the town's dynamic vibe.

Ibiza Town is renowned for its vibrant nightlife, which features a variety of bars and clubs where visitors can dance the night away.

2. On the western coast, San Antonio (Sant Antoni de Portmany) is well known for its sunset strip, where visitors may take in spectacular sunsets and ceremonial drumming. The town's waterfront has a lengthy promenade packed with bars, eateries, and cafes, which fosters a laid-back and social atmosphere. The beaches of San Antonio, like Cala Gració and Cala Salada, have calm waves and a relaxed atmosphere.

Travelers who are looking for a mix of exciting activities and peaceful coastline getaways frequently visit this region.

3. Santa Eulària des Riu: Located on the east coast, Santa Eulària des Riu is well-known for its welcoming attitude for families and gorgeous beaches. The town's picturesque marina, which is surrounded by eateries and stores, is ideal for strolls and boat trips. Cala Llonga and Cala Martina are two serene beaches in Santa Eulària des Riu that are great for water sports and sunbathing. This area is favored by families and couples since it has a laid-back and pleasant atmosphere.

4. Sant Joan de Labritja is a paradise for nature lovers and anyone looking for a quiet escape. It is located in the island's northern countryside.

The region's untamed scenery, which includes rolling hills and forests, makes it an ideal backdrop for hiking and other outdoor pursuits. Sant Joan is a lovely getaway that exudes an original Ibicenco atmosphere.

Travelers who want to get close to nature and enjoy the island's pastoral beauty should visit this area.

5. Sant Josep de sa Talaia: Situated in the southwest of the island, Sant Josep de sa Talaia is a varied landscape that has gorgeous beaches, lovely coves, and beautiful cliffs.

With its classic architecture and inviting town plaza, Sant Josep is a charming place to visit. This area offers a wide variety of coastal experiences, from the well-known Playa d'en Bossa with its energetic beach clubs to the peaceful Cala Vadella and Cala d'Hort with their crystal-clear waters.

6. Rural Inland Regions: Outside of the coastal areas, Ibiza's rural inland regions entice travelers with their tranquil landscapes and quaint settlements. Olive groves, almond orchards, and vineyards decorate the area, which makes for a lovely scene.

Bohemian atmospheres in towns like Santa Gertrudis and Sant Carles de Peralta draw creatives and artists. Away from the tourist hordes, these rural areas provide a chance to discover Ibiza as it truly is.

You will encounter a patchwork of landscapes, cultures, and experiences as you travel through Ibiza's several regions, all of which contribute to the island's alluring character.

The regions of Ibiza offer a variety of options to meet any traveler's preferences, whether they are looking for a dynamic metropolitan lifestyle, idyllic seaside living, or a peaceful country vacation.

CHAPTER 9 : WORTH A SPECIAL TRIP

Hidden Treasures Of Ibiza

Ibiza is well known for its thriving nightlife and stunning beaches, but the island also contains undiscovered gems just waiting to be found by adventurous visitors. These hidden treasures offer a look at the island's less-traveled areas and offer a singular and remarkable experience. We will learn about the Ibiza attractions that are worth a special journey in this chapter.

1. Ses Salines Natural Park is a protected region that includes salt flats, wetlands, and immaculate beaches. It is situated in the southern half of the island.

Discover the ecological richness of the park, see flamingos in the wild, and take in the expansive vistas from the park's watchtowers.

2. Es Amunts: In the northwest of Ibiza, this wild and undeveloped area is a paradise for hikers and nature enthusiasts. Es Amunts offers a taste of the island's unspoiled beauty with its beautiful cliffs, secret coves, and old stone walls.

3. Torre d'en Valls: This watchtower, which is tucked away close to Santa Eulària des Riu, provides stunning views of the area's landscape and shoreline.

The tower, which was built in the 18th century, serves as a reminder of Ibiza's previous fortifications.

4. Atlantis (Sa Pedrera): Atlantis, a legendary and enigmatic location, is a disused quarry close to Cala d'Hort. Its unusual rock formations and serene ponds evoke a surreal ambiance that draws skeptics and nature lovers.

5. Cala Llentrisca is a remote and tranquil inlet on the southwest coast that can only be reached by foot or boat. Its natural beauty makes it the perfect location for a peaceful day of swimming and relaxation.

6. Cap des Falcó: A lesser-known lookout point on the southern extremity of the island, Cap des Falcó is the ideal location to watch the sunset away from the throng. It offers beautiful views of the turquoise sea.

7. Sa Talaia de Sant Josep: Sa Talaia, the highest point on the island, provides sweeping views of the countryside and shoreline of Ibiza. You'll be rewarded for your climb to the summit with breathtaking 360-degree vistas.

Special Qualities and Attractions

Ibiza possesses several distinctive qualities and attractions that distinguish it from other locations in addition to its hidden gems.

Your journey on the island will take on a unique and memorable quality thanks to these one-of-a-kind experiences.

1. Es Vedrà: Off the southwest coast of Ibiza, the mysterious rock island of Es Vedrà is a stunning sight. Es Vedrà, which is surrounded by myths and stories, is thought to possess mystical and magnetic powers that attract both spiritual seekers and artists.

2. Ibiza's vibrant hippy markets are a great place to embrace the island's free-spirited nature. These markets, including Las Dalias and Punta Arab, provide a wide selection of handcrafted goods, apparel, jewelry, and a buzzing creative environment.

3. Ibiza's rich past includes a Phoenician legacy, with relics of this antiquated culture dispersed all across the island. To learn more about Ibiza's past, visit the Phoenician city of Sa Caleta and the Necropolis del Puig des Molins.

4. Ibiza's salt flats have been utilized for producing sea salt for a very long time. Observe Ses Salines' salt ponds' eye-catching pink colors and conventional salt production technique.

5. Carob Trees: Carob trees, a staple of the island's agricultural legacy for many years, may be found all across the countryside of Ibiza.

Discover the carob industry and the many applications for this adaptable Mediterranean plant.

6. Es Culleram Cave: This unusual cave is a long-used site of worship for the goddess Tanit. It is a fascinating and spiritual place to explore because of its ethereal atmosphere and historic carvings.

7. Posidonia Meadows: Ibiza's Posidonia Meadows, a UNESCO World Heritage site, guards the island's maritime ecology. This underwater paradise is accessible to snorkelers and divers, who can also see how crucial it is to preserve the island's coastline health.

8. Boat Excursions: Take a boat tour to find the island's secret coves and remote beaches. Visit Formentera or sail out to see Es Vedrà's mysterious rock formations.

These distinctive qualities and attractions deepen and diversify the Ibiza experience, enhancing your visit and fostering lifelong memories.

CONCLUSION : EMBRACING THE IBIZA EXPERIENCE

Final Thoughts on the Allure of Ibiza

Ibiza has established itself as an island of contrasts thanks to its alluring allure, where a thriving nightlife coexists with tranquil natural beauty and a rich cultural legacy blends with modern vigor. This thorough travel guide has examined Ibiza's attractiveness on many levels, from its famed nightlife and gorgeous beaches to its hidden gems and picture-perfect villages. You have learned more about the island's past, present, and distinctive qualities as you read through the chapters, enabling you to appreciate the variety and depth that Ibiza has to offer to every traveler.

Sustainable and Responsible tourism in Ibiza

It is crucial to adopt sustainable and ethical tourism practices when you set off on your trip to Ibiza.

By being aware of your influence, you can help ensure the sustainability of the island's fragile ecosystems and cultural legacy. Supporting small local businesses, limiting plastic use, and protecting the environment are simple actions that add up to a big impact.

You can help ensure that Ibiza's beauty is preserved for future generations by participating in sustainable activities and supporting programs that place a priority on responsible tourism.

Advice for a Memorable Journey

Here are some suggestions to help you assure a memorable and worthwhile experience as you get ready for your trip to Ibiza:

1. Create an itinerary that meets your interests by researching the island's areas, sights, and activities in advance. Based on your tastes for exciting activities or relaxing getaways, think about the best time to go.

2. Embrace the Culture: Get acquainted with the fascinating traditions, history, and culture of Ibiza. Explore the island's art and music culture, interact with the populace, and eat some native cuisine.

3. Search for Hidden Gems: Go off the beaten road to find Ibiza's hidden gems and secret locations. These less well-known areas might provide distinctive and genuine experiences.

4. Explore with consideration for the environment and the island's history, whether you're hiking through nature preserves, scuba diving, or visiting historical sites.

5. Capture Sunsets: Take in Ibiza's renowned sunsets from a variety of vantage points, allowing the majesty of these mesmerizing moments to envelop you.

6. Engage in outdoor activities like hiking, kayaking, or stand-up paddleboarding to get a close-up view of the island's natural splendor.

7. Experience the Nightlife: To obtain a well-rounded sense of the island's entertainment scene, enjoy Ibiza's lively nightlife while also looking for quaint pubs and cultural events.

8. Ibiza is known for its magnetic Es Vedrà rock, vibrant hippy markets, and Phoenician history, which help to define the island's unique characteristics.

9. Consider Staying in Unique Accommodations: To enjoy the island's varied hospitality offers, think about staying in rural hotels, rustic retreats, or eco-friendly lodges.

10. Embrace Sustainability: help eco-friendly companies and exercise mindfulness when visiting Ibiza to help the island's efforts to promote sustainable tourism.

Let Ibiza's dynamic energy, breathtaking scenery, and diverse culture immerse you as soon as you step foot on the enchanted island. Ibiza provides a multitude of activities just waiting to be enjoyed, from the vibrant nightlife to the serene countryside.

Ibiza welcomes you with open arms whether you're looking for adventure, relaxation, or immersion in cultural delights.

Create treasured memories that will last long after you leave this Mediterranean paradise by accepting its allure, valuing its hidden gems, and embracing it.

Good luck and may your trip to Ibiza be full of wonder, joy, and soul-stirring experiences.

Printed in Great Britain
by Amazon